Illustrations by Curtis Brown, Jr.

ISBN: 978-1523242368
ISBN: 1523242361

I dedicate this book to my Universal Princess London. You are my world of laughter.

My Laugh is gone. It came
out of my nose and into
the portal it goes.

I ran into the portal and I
flipped and twirled. I saw a
sign that read "Welcome
to Laugh World".

There were Laughs everywhere. Some big and round. Some were jumping up and down. Some were flying with little jet packs. Some were playing with baseball bats.

Some were swinging. Some were
singing. Some were sitting
on the bench reading.

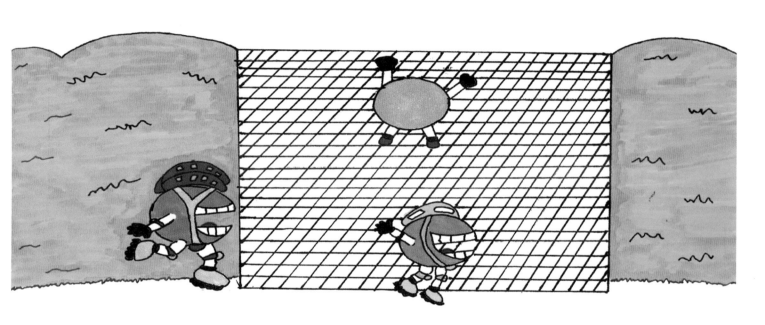

There were Laughs that skate and some climbing gates. All the Laughs love to play.

Then I heard a voice that was deep and mellow. The voice said,"How are you little fellow?" I turned around and he was standing behind with a crown on his head and a red bowtie. I replied: "I am fine. Who are you with a crown that shine?"

"I am King Laugh. King of Laugh World. I make sure that laughs go to all boys and girls."

We have Laughs of all different
colors and sizes. Some that are
sneaky. Some with surprises.

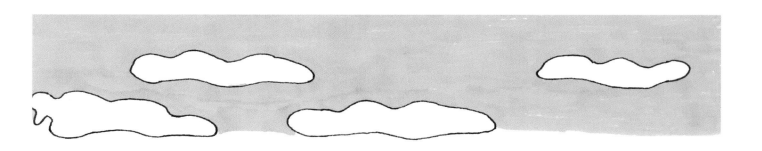

Some that jump rope. Some that row boats. We even have some that play practical jokes.

Yes we have Laughs for miles and miles. Tell me, what are you doing in our little laugh town?

Well, I lost my Laugh. I don't see
it anywhere. Maybe the Frowns
took it over there.

Who are the Frowns? They are mean and bad. They don't like the Laughs. They want kids to be sad.

Well, I'll go to Frown Land to get my Laugh back! King Laugh said, "I can help you with that." We'll go together and bring your friend. She'll help us get your Laugh back again.

WELCOME
TO
LAUGH WORLD

Hi! I'm King Laugh. I hope you enjoyed your stay at Laugh World. I was happy to help Camden find his laugh, but he wasn't here. Camden is still on a quest to find his laugh. Stay tuned to find out if Camden will find his Laugh in Frown Land. I can't wait see you there!